THE O
TOTTENHAM HOTSPUR
ANNUAL 2018

TOTTENHAM HOTSPUR

Written by Michael Bridge
Designed by Chris Dalrymple

A Grange Publication

©2017. Published by Grange Communications Ltd., Edinburgh, under licence from Tottenham Hotspur Ltd. Printed in the EU.

Photography © PA Images.

ISBN 978-1-911287-81-0

CONTENTS

WELCOME

Dear Supporters,

Welcome to the 2018 Official Tottenham Hotspur Annual.

For the second successive season we secured Champions League football after finishing second in the Premier League – our highest finish since 1963. It was a season to remember as we said goodbye to White Hart Lane in style, winning 17 out of the 19 home league games.

As you can see with the latest images on our website, our new stadium is beginning to take shape in what is an extremely exciting few years for the Club. Wembley is our temporary home for the current season and once again we thank you for your terrific support week in, week out.

It's now Mauricio Pochettino's fourth season at the Club and we've seen real progress every year. It's a squad with a perfect blend of youth and experience. Harry Kane won the Premier League Golden Boot Award for the second successive season and Dele Alli retained the PFA Young Player of the Year Award. Congratulations to them both.

In this Annual, you'll be able to relive a memorable day as we beat Manchester United 2-1 in our final game at White Hart Lane. We have player profiles of all your favourite players, plus a look at a number of our youngsters looking to impress Mauricio Pochettino in 2018. There's a definitive profile of all our new signings too. We also have a number of quizzes to test your knowledge of Spurs.

Thank you for your continued support.
Enjoy your new Annual.
Come on you Spurs!

Michael Bridge

SEASON REVIEW

What an incredible 2016/2017 season for Spurs. We finished second on 86 points – our highest league placing since 1963 and our biggest ever points total to once again secure Champions League football. We also said goodbye to White Hart Lane in style, ending the season at our famous old stadium unbeaten, winning 17 League games out of a possible 19. Dele Alli won the PFA Young Player of the Year for the second successive season while Harry Kane retained the Premier League Golden Boot after 29 goals in 30 League games.

August

We started the season with a trip to Goodison Park. Eric Lamela's fantastic header earned us a point on the opening day. Victor Wanyama, on his home debut, scored the only goal of the game against Crystal Palace in our first game of the season at White Hart Lane. Seven days later, we earned a point at home to Liverpool, Danny Rose with our equaliser.

September

We started September in impressive fashion, beating Stoke 4-0 at the Bet365 Stadium. Two goals from the excellent Heung-Min Son, and one each from Dele Alli and Harry Kane saw us return to London with three points. It was a mixed afternoon against Sunderland as Harry Kane scored the only goal of the game but was later substituted after suffering ankle ligament damage. Life without Kane started well; Heung-Min Son turned in a man of the match performance scoring both goals in a 2-1 win over Middlesbrough.

October

One of our best performances of the season came against Manchester City, who at the time were unbeaten and looked unstoppable. A Kolarov own goal, and one from Dele Alli, secured an excellent 2-0 win. It wasn't so easy a week later, as we needed a Dele stoppage time goal to earn a point at West Brom. We then travelled to Bournemouth in what was a hard fought goalless draw. We ended the month with a home game against champions Leicester, Vincent Janssen scored a penalty but we were held to a 1-1 draw in a frustrating game.

November

The north London derby at the Emirates saw the return of Harry Kane, and it didn't take him long to get back amongst the goals as he scored a penalty to put us ahead. Arsenal levelled late on, but couldn't find a winner as our good recent form against our rivals continued. In what was a month of derbies, the next was a memorable one as West Ham arrived in N17. It was a day to remember for Harry Winks, as he scored his first goal for the Club. Trailing 2-1 and heading into stoppage time, Harry Kane scored an equaliser, but there was still time for him to score a last gasp penalty to win an amazing game. Our final derby of the month saw us lose narrowly at Chelsea – Christian Eriksen put us ahead with an incredible goal but we left Stamford Bridge pointless in our first league defeat of the season.

December

We started the Christmas period with a comprehensive victory over Swansea City. Harry Kane and Christian Eriksen both scored twice; Heung-Min Son added another in a dominant performance. A week later, in a game of very few chances, Manchester United scored the only goal of the game on a frustrating afternoon at Old Trafford. That disappointment was short-lived as we beat Hull City 3-0 just three days later, Christian Eriksen (2) and Victor Wanyama with the goals. Burnley were the next visitors to White Hart Lane. After they took the lead, Dele Alli levelled for Spurs, before a Danny Rose winner on 71 minutes. December ended in stunning fashion as we thrashed Southampton 4-1 at St Mary's; two from the in-form Dele Alli and one each from Harry Kane and Heung-Min Son sealed a brilliant win.

January

It was a very happy New Year's Day at Vicarage Road as we replicated our scoreline at Southampton with Dele Alli once again the man of the moment. He and Harry Kane both scored twice to continue what was a fantastic Christmas period for Spurs. Things were about to get even better as we beat an in-form Chelsea side 2-0 at White Hart Lane to deny Chelsea a 14th successive Premier League victory. Perhaps the most dominant performance came ten days later, as the crowd were on their feet to applaud a stunning hat-trick from Harry Kane in a 4-0 win over West Brom. At this point, Spurs were irresistible. Goals from Dele and Heung-Min Son earned a valuable point at the Etihad Stadium but we ended the month with a frustrating draw at Sunderland. Danny Rose suffered a knee injury that would keep him out for the rest of the season.

February

A Harry Kane penalty was enough to earn three points in a hard-fought win over Middlesbrough at White Hart Lane. Our worst performance of the League season came a week later at Liverpool, as we were beaten 2-0. In a month dominated by cup competitions, we ended February on a high note, with an excellent 4-0 win over Stoke City. Harry Kane scored a brilliant first half hat-trick, and Dele Alli was also on target a minute into the second half.

March

It was the Harry and Dele show once again as Kane's two goals and one from Alli helped us to beat Everton 3-2 at White Hart Lane. We ended the month with yet another home win, and another goal from Dele, as we beat Southampton 2-1 – Christian Eriksen scoring the opener.

April

We started off the month in style, as goals from Eric Dier and Heung-Min Son earned a 2-0 win at Burnley. Four days later, we made the long trip to Swansea, and it looked like we were heading for defeat until goals from Dele, Heung-Min Son and Christian Eriksen, in six crazy minutes, earned us an unlikely yet memorable win. We continued to dominate at home, as Watford found out. Goals from Dele, Eric Dier and two from Heung-Min Son sealed a comfortable 4-0 win. The goals just kept on coming as we matched the score-line against Bournemouth the following week; Mousa Dembele, Heung-Min Son, Harry Kane and Vincent Janssen all on target. Four days after disappointment in the FA Cup semi-final, we kept our title hopes alive with a hard-fought win at Crystal Palace, Christian Eriksen with the winner. Two goals in two second half minutes from Dele and Harry Kane ensured victory in the last ever north London derby at White Hart Lane, and our 13th straight win at home. The win also meant we were guaranteed to finish above our north London rivals.

May

Our title hopes took a huge dent at the London Stadium as West Ham ran out 1-0 winners, much to the delight of the home support. That disappointment was soon forgotten with what will forever be one of the most memorable games in the Club's history as we said goodbye to White Hart Lane. Victor Wanyama and Harry Kane were our goal-scorers as we beat Manchester United 2-1 in a fitting finale and extended our run to 17 wins in 19 games, remaining unbeaten at White Hart Lane all season. The win also secured second spot in the Premier League. With second already secured you could forgive the players for downing tools, however this kind of attitude does not exist under Mauricio Pochettino, as we quite clearly showed in our last two games of the season. Firstly, we demolished Leicester 6-1 with four goals coming from Harry Kane and two from Heung-Min Son. We didn't just equal that scoreline, we bettered it just three days later with a phenomenal 7-1 win at Hull City. Three more for hero Harry meant he retained the Premier League's Golden Boot, despite missing a big chunk of the season through injury. Dele, Victor Wanyama, Ben Davies and Toby Alderweireld completed the rout. Kane's performance was so impressive that he was given a standing ovation by the home supporters. It completed a season to remember for the Club, as we finished second on 86 points – our highest league placing since 1963 and our biggest ever points total. While we have been lucky to have witnessed some fantastic teams throughout the decades, there is no doubt this current crop are right up there.

CHAMPIONS LEAGUE REVIEW

Group E

Spurs 1-2 Monaco

Our return to Champions League football ended in a disappointing fashion as Monaco ran out 2-1 winners in front of over 85,000 fans at Wembley Stadium. Toby Alderweireld pulled a goal back for Spurs but we couldn't recover from a poor start. Despite defeat, there were many records broken on the night:

The final figure of 85,011 became our record home attendance, surpassing our previous mark of 75,038 set for an FA Cup sixth round tie against Sunderland at White Hart Lane on 5 March 1938.

But that's not all…

The figure of 85,011 was the highest attendance for a home match for an English club.

We also toppled the previous best of 84,569 held by Manchester City for an FA Cup tie against Stoke at Maine Road in 1934.

Our 85,011 attendance is the highest by an English club for a home match in the Champions League.

CSKA Moscow 0-1 Spurs

Heung-Min Son's goal on 71 minutes earned Spurs a deserved win as we dominated in Russia to secure our first points in the group.

Bayer Leverkusen 0-0 Spurs

We returned to England with a point after an entertaining goalless draw in Germany. Vincent Janssen had a goal disallowed and later hit the bar, while Bayer also wondered how they didn't score as we had Hugo Lloris to thank as the ball looked to be going in the back of the net but he somehow dragged it along the line.

Spurs 0-1 Bayer Leverkusen

Records were broken yet again as a crowd of 85,512 turned up to see Leverkusen claim all three points on a hugely frustrating night at Wembley. Kevin Kampl put Leverkusen ahead on 65 minutes and despite our best efforts, we couldn't find an equaliser to leave ourselves with a lot to do to advance to the last 16.

Monaco 2-1 Spurs

Five crazy minutes at the Stade Louis II ended our involvement in the Champions League. Djibril Sidibe put Monaco ahead, Harry Kane's penalty made it 1-1 but Monaco won it just one minute later through Thomas Lemar. Hugo Lloris also saved a first half Radamel Falcao penalty.

Spurs 3-1 CSKA Moscow

Our campaign ended on a positive note as we secured 3rd spot and a place in the Europa League with a comfortable win over CSKA Moscow. After falling behind, Dele Alli levelled, Harry Kane put us in front a minute into the second half and an Akinfeev own goal sealed a 3-1 win.

UEFA EUROPA LEAGUE REVIEW

Europa League round of 32

Gent 1-0 Spurs

Jeremy Perbet's second half strike against the run of play gave the Belgian side a first leg advantage with the return leg at Wembley just seven days away.

Spurs 2-2 Gent

Our involvement in the Europa League was over after Gent's late equaliser was too much to turn around. It started so well, too, as Christian Eriksen put us ahead after 10 minutes with a clever finish. Gent equalised on 20 minutes before a Victor Wanyama goal put us back in front in the second half. But Dele Alli's first half sending off resulted in tired legs as the game approached the latter stages and Gent took advantage to earn a place in the last 16.

FA CUP REVIEW

3rd round – Spurs 2-0 Aston Villa

A much-changed Spurs side eventually saw off Aston Villa with goals from Ben Davies, his first for the Club and Heung Min-Son. Harry Winks started and was named man of the match with an impressive display from midfield, with his superb range of passing catching the eye.

4th round – Spurs 4-3 Wycombe

In an incredible match at White Hart Lane, it took a 97th, minute winner from Sonny to seal our place in the fifth round and avoid a replay. It was heading to be one of the biggest FA Cup shocks for some time as Wycombe went into the second half 2-0 ahead to stun the White Hart Lane crowd. Son pulled a goal back before Vincent Janssen's penalty made it 2-2. On 83 minutes, the League Two side were back in front through Garry Thompson. Spurs went on all-out attack now and substitute Dele Alli's clever finish looked to have earned a replay before Heung-Min Son broke Wycombe hearts with a late, late goal.

5th round – Fulham 0-3 Spurs

If the Wycombe win was slightly fortunate, victory at Fulham was quite the opposite, as a superb Harry Kane hat-trick sent us through to the quarter-final. Our football was sublime at times against a well organised Fulham side. Kane, wearing the captain's armband, was clinical, scoring just before half time and two more in front of the Spurs fans in the second half.

6th round – Spurs 6-0 Millwall

Heung-Min Son was the hat-trick hero in the quarter-final as we made sure there was to be no repeat of the Wycombe match with a comprehensive win over League One Millwall. However, it was a start to forget for Spurs as Harry Kane limped off with an ankle injury. It didn't affect the side, though as a Christian Eriksen effort put Spurs ahead. Heung-Min Son was simply unplayable and deserved his hat-trick. Dele Alli and Vincent Janssen completed the scoring to book a place in the semi-final.

Semi-final – Chelsea 4-2 Spurs

Before the match, there was a minute's applause for our Under-23s coach, Ugo Ehiogu, who sadly passed away just two days before the match. Chelsea ended our participation in the competition as two quick goals settled this semi-final. After falling behind, Harry Kane levelled with an excellent header. Dele Alli made it 2-2 in the second half but goals from Eden Hazard and an unstoppable effort from Nemanja Matic sealed Chelsea's place in the final.

EFL CUP REVIEW

3rd round – Spurs 5-0 Gillingham

On an enjoyable night at White Hart Lane, a mixture of First Team and youth combined to beat League One Gillingham with ease. Christian Eriksen, captain on the night, scored twice, his first a stunning effort. Vincent Janssen scored his first goal for the Club along with Joshua Onomah. Erik Lamela was also on target.

4th round – Liverpool 2-1 Spurs

Our League Cup run came to an end at the fourth round stage after a narrow defeat at Anfield. Once again Mauricio Pochettino made wholesale changes to the starting XI. Daniel Sturridge scored both goals for Liverpool, while Vincent Janssen scored from the penalty spot for Spurs. Despite defeat, it was another run out for the likes of Harry Winks, Cameron Carter-Vickers, Joshua Onomah and a great debut for Shayon Harrison.

SUPER SPURS STATS 2016/2017

Second place is our highest finish in the Premier League era and our best since 1962/1963.

The all-time record 7-1 away win at Hull on the final day took us to 26 wins, five more than our previous best of 21 set in 2009/2010, 2012/2013 and 2013/2014.

Four defeats is our lowest not just in the Premier League, but also a new Club best in the top-flight. It matches four defeats set all the way back in 1919/1920 in the old Second Division.

13 goals in our final two matches eclipsed our previous best number of strikes in the Premier League, which was last season's 69, making it 86 overall.

26 goals conceded is a new Club best. That beat our previous best of 35 in the Premier League set last season and 33 in a top-flight season, set in the old First Division in 1970/1971.

Plus 60 goal difference eclipsed our previous best of plus-34 set last season.

86 points betters our previous best of 72 in the Premier League set in 2012/2013.

Final table 2016/2017									
Pos	Team	Pld	W	D	L	GF	GA	GD	Pts
1	Chelsea	38	30	3	5	85	33	52	93
2	Tottenham	38	26	8	4	86	26	60	86
3	Man. City	38	23	9	6	80	39	41	78
4	Liverpool	38	22	10	6	78	42	36	76
5	Arsenal	38	23	6	9	77	44	33	75
6	Man United	38	18	15	5	54	28	25	69
7	Everton	38	17	10	11	62	44	18	61
8	Southampton	38	12	10	16	41	48	-7	46
9	Bournemouth	38	12	10	16	55	67	-12	46
10	West Brom	38	12	9	17	43	51	-8	45
11	West Ham	38	12	9	17	47	64	-17	45
12	Leicester City	38	12	8	18	48	63	-15	44
13	Stoke City	38	11	11	16	41	56	-15	44
14	Crystal Palace	38	12	5	21	50	63	-13	41
15	Swansea City	38	12	5	21	45	70	-25	41
16	Burnley FC	38	11	7	20	39	55	-16	40
17	Watford	38	11	7	20	40	68	-28	40
R	Hull City	38	9	7	22	37	80	-43	34
R	Middlesbrough	38	5	13	20	27	53	-26	28
R	Sunderland	38	6	6	26	29	69	-40	24

"HARRY KANE, HE'S ONE OF OUR OWN!"

If there was any lingering doubt about Harry Kane's place amongst the world's elite, it was sensationally removed after another stunning campaign resulting in a second successive Premier League Golden Boot despite two serious ankle injuries.

Harry scored 17 goals in 20 appearances for the Under-18s in his first full season in the Academy in 2009/2010 and hasn't looked back since. Kane finished last season on 99 club goals in total. May and June 2017 will live long in the memory of the popular striker. His final two hat-tricks in the final two games of the season at Leicester and Hull helped secure the Premier League's Golden Boot for the second-successive season. It got even better for Harry after he was awarded the England captaincy for games against Scotland and France. Harry scored a dramatic equaliser at Hampden, and a further two in France made it the perfect end to the season on a personal note for Kane.

It looked highly unlikely for Harry to win a second Golden Boot. Trailing behind Alexis Sanchez and Romelu Lukaku with three games to go, but eight goals in three games (yes, eight in three!) secured the award.

Harry's hat-tricks

Harry is now up to eight hat-tricks* for Spurs, only the great Jimmy Greaves (15), Bobby Smith (12), George Hunt (11), Johnny Morrison (10) and Cliff Jones (10) have scored more. Harry hit an incredible FIVE hat-tricks during the season, equalling a Club record alongside George Hunt (1933/1934) and Johnny Morrison (1936/1937).

Ankle woe didn't stop Harry

Harry suffered an ankle injury against Sunderland in September 2016, ruling him out of action for two months. He returned in style, scoring a penalty at Arsenal in November. He went on to score two a week later at home to West Ham and was clinical during our Christmas fixtures at Southampton and Watford, both 4-1 victories. A hat-trick against Stoke and another two against Everton kept our title challenge alive but another ankle ligament injury, this time against Millwall put participation for the title run-in in serious doubt. Remarkably, Harry returned just three weeks later, making a late substitute appearance against Watford at White Hart Lane. Harry featured in the final eight games, scoring in six of them, but his goals at Leicester and Hull made it 11 goals in eight games after his injury.

> **I've got to give big thanks to the team, they create so many chances and I've just got to make sure I'm in the positions to put them away.**
>
> **Thanks, lads**

*at time of publication

Fact:

Last season, Harry became only the second Spurs player to win the Golden Boot back-to-back, following the great Jimmy Greaves over 50 years ago.

Harry Kane became only the third Spur to score five hat-tricks in a season in 2016/2017 - and the first in 80 years.

Harry is already a Spurs hero and has targeted another season full of goals. Typical of the man, he was quick to mention the efforts of his teammates, insisting none of this would be possible without them.

"I had a couple of setbacks last season with injuries but they only made me stronger. I've got to give big thanks to the team, they create so many chances and I've just got to make sure I'm in the positions to put them away. Sonny, Dele, Christian, the boys at the back and Hugo, the midfield securing everything up and Trips (Kieran Trippier) and Ben putting in the deliveries, it's a dream to play for this team. Without them, I wouldn't be holding awards."

To top it all off, Harry won the PFA Fans' Premier League Player of the Season prize. With the winner decided by the general public, over 49,000 votes were cast, with Harry coming out on top with 16,378 votes. The football world has their eyes on Harry but he's relishing the pressure. Tottenham Hotspur's key man and England captain is raring to go, hoping to make 2018 even better than 2017.

Tottenham Hotspur's Goal-den boys

Spurs players to finish top goalscorer in the top flight

1957/1958	Bobby Smith 36 goals in Division One
1962/1963	Jimmy Greaves 37 goals in Division One
1963/1964	Jimmy Greaves 35 goals in Division One
1964/1965	Jimmy Greaves 29 goals in Division One (tied with Andy McEvoy, Blackburn)
1968/1969	Jimmy Greaves 27 goals in Division One
1980/1981	Steve Archibald 20 goals in Division One (tied with Peter Withe, Villa)
1986/1987	Clive Allen 33 goals in Division One (record 49 for a Spurs season, also won European Golden Boot as the top league goalscorer across all European leagues)
1989/1990	Gary Lineker 24 goals in Division One
1992/1993	Teddy Sheringham 22 goals (21 for us, one for Forest) in Premier League - introduction of PL Golden Boot, first winner.
2015/2016	Harry Kane 25 goals in Premier League
2016/2017	Harry Kane 29 goals in the Premier League (highest total for us in a PL season)

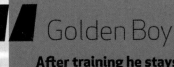

Golden Boy

After training he stays behind, doing shooting practice all the time. He fully deserves his Golden Boot and hopefully he'll get a third one this season.

Kieran Trippier on Harry Kane

OUR GREAT DANE

One Hotspur Members Player of the Season
Supporters' Clubs Player of the Season

It was hard to select an individual last season after a stunning campaign. Harry Kane retained the Premier League Golden Boot, Dele Alli retained the PFA Young Player of the Year award, Danny Rose in the PFA Team of the Year, Super Heung-Min Son's goals, Toby Alderweireld at the back, but our supporters decided Christian Eriksen was our standout performer.

The Denmark international was an integral part of Mauricio Pochettino's team last term, scoring 12 goals and a remarkable 21 assists in 47 appearances. In fact, it's the second time he has completed the Club awards 'double' after his first season in 2013/2014.

"There have been a few players - in fact most of the team - who had an incredible season but I'm very pleased the fans voted for me and it meant a lot.", said Christian.

Despite 2016/2017 being our best-ever campaign in the Premier League, Christian echoed the thoughts of the rest of the squad by demanding an even better 2018.

"We have a great squad. We know can have great success here. We want success for our fans, too. They all deserve a lot of credit for the way they help push the team throughout the season and hopefully that will carry on. You can see the way the Club is moving with the new stadium and we'll have a lot more fans in there and hopefully an even better atmosphere."

In May last year, Christian became the first player in the Premier League to register over 100 chances created for his teammates. He also had 84 of his shots saved in the Premier League last season; more than any other player. Including this on top of his brilliant goals and assists record last season, it's widely considered he's now up there as one of the best attacking midfielders in world football.

Christian's crackers

Spurs 5-0 Gillingham – Captain for the night, Christian unleashed an unstoppable 25-yard strike to open the scoring. Classic Christian!

Chelsea 2-1 Spurs – Despite being on the losing side, Christian opened the scoring with a brilliant half-volley with his left foot outside the area leaving Thibaut Courtois with little chance.

Crystal Palace 0-1 Spurs - Christian's fierce low drive at Selhurst Park earned us a crucial win. The strike finished second in our Goal of the Season awards.

Born: 14 February 1992
Position: Midfielder
Joined Spurs: 30 August 2013
Height (m): 1.82
Weight (kg): 76
Previous Club(s): Ajax
Squad number: 23

DELE ALLI

From a youngster at MK Dons to one of the biggest talents in world football in under three years, Dele Alli continues to make huge strides under Mauricio Pochettino. The popular attacking midfielder is now in his third season at the Club and he's loving every minute of it. Dele hopes to end 2017/2018 with Club success; the England international is used to individual honours after retaining the PFA Young Player of the Year award for 2017. Dele enjoyed a stunning campaign, scoring 22 goals in his 50 appearances in all competitions, including 18 in 37 in the Premier League. He was also named One Hotspur Junior Members Player of the Season for the second-successive season. With individual honours coming to him regularly, Dele was quick to point out the impact the Spurs supporters have made during his time at the Club.

"I think that's one thing we have got here, the support is unbelievable, the fans at the games as well as the ones who can't make it and are supporting us all around the world.

"They all deserve a lot of credit for the way they help push the team throughout the season and hopefully that will carry on. You can see the way the Club is moving with the new stadium and we'll have a lot more fans in there and hopefully an even better atmosphere."

For now the home is Wembley, a stadium Dele is used to for club and country. A big stage for a player who thrives on the big occasion. He'll never forget his first England goal at the national stadium, a 25-yard effort on his full debut. A man of many goals, and, after scoring 22 last season, one stood out to win our Goal of the Season. His fine strike against Watford in April 2017 won the award.

Speaking about his strike against Watford, Dele said: "Once you catch a ball sweetly you know it has a good chance of going in and as soon as I hit that one I knew it was going to test the keeper at least, and thankfully it went in."

Great goals are certainly part of Dele's game, who could possibly forget his incredible strike at Crystal Palace in his first season at Spurs. 10 goals in his first season at the Club was extremely impressive, but 18 in his second has led to many considering Dele to be one of the hottest young talents around, but typically of Dele, he isn't getting carried away.

"I've still got to improve on putting my chances away, so I'll keep working on that. But there's a lot of little bits that need improving.", he added.

Asked for the highlight of his brilliant season, Dele replied: "There were a lot. The main one's probably Chelsea at home, when we won 2-0, just because there was a lot that went into that game."

> I'm extremely proud. It's a great honour for me - obviously the second year in a row - but I've still got a lot to do, I've got to keep working hard. I've got to keep improving.
> Dele on retaining the PFA award

PFA YOUNG PLAYER OF THE YEAR REPRESENTING SPURS
1979-80 Glenn Hoddle, **2011-12** Kyle Walker,
2012-13 Gareth Bale, **2014-15** Harry Kane,
2015-16 Dele Alli, **2016-17** Dele Alli

MAURICIO POCHETTINO

Spurs continue to make great strides under Mauricio Pochettino. League records were broken when we challenged Leicester in 2015/2016, ultimately finishing third, but we went one better under Mauricio last season, finishing second for the first time since 1962/1963, and Club best records were broken again, but this time in every Premier League category.

Most wins – 26   Fewest defeats – 4
Most goals – 86   Fewest conceded – 26
Best goal difference +60   Most points - 86

Despite the phenomenal records broken, remarkably it still wasn't enough to win the Premier League title. There was great disappointment at the end of season 2015/2016, a 5-1 defeat at Newcastle but the same couldn't be said in May 2017 as we said goodbye to White Hart Lane with a 2-1 win over Manchester United and we followed that up with 6-1 and 7-1 victories at Leicester and Hull respectively. Despite league rivals once again strengthening in the summer, Mauricio refused to rest and challenged the squad to continue to improve.

"Our dream and our challenge is to be better. Now is a moment to take decisions, to try to improve and try to provide the team with all the tools to try to win, that's the challenge for us always."

Now in his fourth season at the Club, the squad Mauricio has built has the perfect balance of youth and experience.

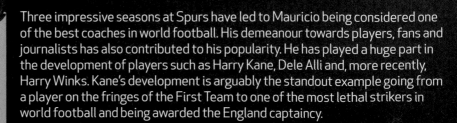

I'm so proud, the way we finished last season was fantastic. I think to be second in the table, fighting all the way on 86 points, it was amazing.

Three impressive seasons at Spurs have led to Mauricio being considered one of the best coaches in world football. His demeanour towards players, fans and journalists has also contributed to his popularity. He has played a huge part in the development of players such as Harry Kane, Dele Alli and, more recently, Harry Winks. Kane's development is arguably the standout example going from a player on the fringes of the First Team to one of the most lethal strikers in world football and being awarded the England captaincy.

Despite admiration away from N17, Pochettino's commitment and love for the Club is stronger than ever. There is plenty to look forward to on and off the pitch. Managing the Club on the opening of our fantastic new stadium is just one of many targets for the Argentinian and if the squad that Poch built continues to improve, it won't be long before he'll have his hands on silverware.

MEET OUR BACKROOM TEAM:

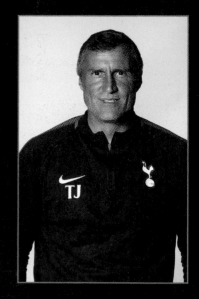

Jesus Perez – Assistant Manager

Jesus followed 'Poch' to Spurs in May 2014 after a successful spell as Southampton Assistant Manager. Jesus also worked alongside him at Espanyol as Fitness Coach. Born in Spain, Jesus has coached for 18 years at Al Ittihad, Almeria, Rayo Vallecano, Pontevedra, Real Murcia, Castellon and Tarragona.

Miguel D'Agostino – First Team Coach

Miguel, like Jesus, followed Mauricio Pochettino to White Hart Lane from Southampton. He played alongside Pochettino for Argentinian side Newell's Old Boys in the early 1990s. After leaving French side Brest as Chief Scout, he joined Pochettino's coaching staff at Espanyol.

Toni Jiménez – Goalkeeping Coach

After leaving Barcelona, Toni had a brief spell at Rayo Vallecano, before making over 200 appearances for Espanyol, where he met then team-mate Mauricio Pochettino. Toni won three caps for Spain and won a gold medal for Spain in the 1992 Olympics. He returned to Espanyol as Assistant Coach to Mauricio, before following him to Southampton.

Wayne Burnett – Under-23 Coach

Wayne joined Spurs at the beginning of pre-season. The former Dagenham & Redbridge manager represented Leyton Orient, Blackburn Rovers, Plymouth Argyle, Bolton Wanderers, Huddersfield Town and Grimsby Town – making over 100 appearances for the latter two clubs – during an extensive playing career in the Football League. He left his post as Dagenham & Redbridge manager in December 2015, and has since worked as a National Coach Developer at the Football Association.

Scott Parker – Under-18 Coach

Scotty needs no introduction to the Spurs faithful. A former England international, Scott gave us two seasons of tremendous service as a player between 2011 and 2013, making 63 appearances in all competitions. He spent the last four years at Fulham, where he served as club captain before announcing his retirement from playing at the end of last season. Earlier in his career, Scott represented Charlton Athletic, Norwich City (on loan), Chelsea, Newcastle United and West Ham United. He won 18 senior England caps and skippered the Three Lions for one match during his time here at Spurs.

PLAYER PROFILES

HUGO LLORIS

Our Club captain is now in his sixth season at the Club. Hugo featured on 43 occasions last season after quickly recovering from a hamstring injury at the start of the campaign. Regarded as one of the best goalkeepers in the world, Hugo kept 15 clean sheets for Spurs to help us finish runners-up.

MICHEL VORM

Dutch international goalkeeper joined us from Swansea in the summer of 2014. Michel made 11 appearances last season for Spurs including our draw against Liverpool in August 2016 where he made a number of superb saves.

PAULO GAZZANIGA

Paulo joined us from Southampton in August 2017, signing a contract with the Club until 2022. Paulo, a product of Valencia's youth setup, left Spain for Gillingham in July 2011, before joining Southampton a year later, where he went on to work with Mauricio Pochettino and his coaching staff. He made 23 appearances for the Saints before spending the 2016/2017 season on loan at Spanish side Rayo Vallecano, where he played 22 times.

KIERAN TRIPPIER

Kieran joined Spurs from Burnley in June 2015. Last season saw Kieran establish himself as our first choice right back as the campaign came to an end. His form earned him an England call-up and was impressive against France in June 2016.

JAN VERTONGHEN

Now in his sixth season at the Club, Jan is a key member of the team. His performances earned him a new contract last season and he continues to enjoy an excellent partnership with fellow Belgian Toby Alderweireld. Jan is also a regular in the Belgium team and is now close to 100 caps for his country.

TOBY ALDERWEIRELD

A top class defender, Toby remains a tremendous presence at the back alongside Jan Vertonghen. A knee injury in October meant Toby missed a chunk of our season but still featured on 39 occasions. He also scored on the last day of the season in our 7-1 victory at already-relegated Hull City.

BEN
DAVIES

Ben enjoyed a superb second half of the season. After injury to Danny Rose, Ben featured heavily and was a regular on our left hand side, often being used as a wing back and this position saw him score twice. Ben's form earned him a new long term contract with the Club. Ben continues to be a key part of the Welsh national side.

DANNY
ROSE

Despite suffering a knee injury at the end of January to keep him out for the rest of the season, Danny did enough to earn himself a spot in the PFA Team of the Season for the second successive year. Danny has now been at the Club for over 10 years after arriving from Leeds in July 2007 and is the first choice left back for England too when fit.

KYLE
WALKER-PETERS

Kyle joined the First Team ranks in the summer after an impressive pre-season. He made his senior debut from the start in a 2-0 win at Newcastle United on the opening weekend of the 2017/2018 Premier League season. He received the man of the match award to cap off a perfect day. The England Under-21 international was rewarded with a new contract in August 2017.

DAVINSON SANCHEZ

Davinson joined Spurs from Ajax in August 2017. The Colombia international moved to Ajax from Colombian club Atletico Nacional in June, 2016, and made 47 appearances for the Dutch side, scoring seven goals. He won Ajax's 'Rinus Michels' Player of the Year Award in his only season at the Club, which was previously won by Jan Vertonghen in 2012 and Rafael van der Vaart in 2002.

JUAN FOYTH

Juan became our third summer signing after completing his move from Estudiantes in August 2017. The 19-year-old defender has signed a contract with the Club until 2022. Having established himself in Estudiantes' First Team, Juan has represented Argentina at Under-20 level 12 times and was a key member of their 2017 FIFA Under-20 World Cup and 2017 Under-20 South American Championship squads. Juan has quickly made an impression and is a regular in the First Team squad.

SERGE AURIER

Serge joined Spurs on deadline day from PSG. The powerful full back is highly rated in France and left the club a huge success, winning two Ligue 1 titles, three French Cups, three French League Cups and four French Super Cups. The Ivory Coast international was selected in the 2015 African Cup of Nations Team of the Tournament when his country lifted the trophy. (Annual went to print before player appeared in Spurs shirt.)

ERIC DIER

Eric's versatility makes him a very important member of the team. Often used as a defensive midfielder for club and country in 2016, Eric moved to a back three alongside Jan and Toby for us last season. Eric scored two goals in 46 appearances, captaining us for the first time at Liverpool in the EFL Cup in October 2016, and then captaining the side in the early rounds of our run to the FA Cup semi-finals.

MOUSA DEMBÉLÉ

Despite minor injuries and a suspension at the start of the season, Mousa still played an important role as we secured second place in the Premier League. Mousa made 39 appearances and scored in our 4-0 win over Bournemouth. The Belgium international formed a formidable partnership with Victor Wanyama to help us secure an unbeaten record in our final season at White Hart Lane.

VICTOR WANYAMA

A stunning first season at Spurs. Victor immediately impressed the fans with his strength and tough tackling. He scored on his home debut in the 1-0 win over Crystal Palace, and he had started every game before suffering a back injury at Burnley in April. Goals aren't usually a main part of his game but he found the net against Manchester United in our final game at White Hart Lane and in both games against Hull City.

HARRY WINKS

Harry impressed coaching staff and supporters last season and has already shown maturity way beyond his years. The England Under-21s international scored his first goal for the Club against West Ham. Harry continued to feature for the First Team until he suffered a serious ankle injury at Burnley ruling him out for the rest of the season but has returned to the side and continues to shine with his spectacular passing from midfield.

DELE ALLI

For the second successive season, Dele was named PFA Young Player of the Year and earned a spot in the PFA Premier League Team of the Year. Dele is now considered one of the biggest talents in world football. Dele broke the 20-goal barrier with 22 in total, helping us earn a runners-up spot in the league. Plus, he won our Supporters' Clubs Goal of the Season prize for the second year in a row, this time for his cracker against Watford at White Hart Lane in April 2017. Perhaps his most memorable moment of the season was against Chelsea in January 2017, as his two headers earned us a 2-0 win.

MOUSSA SISSOKO

French international attacking midfielder joined Spurs on deadline day in August 2016 from Newcastle United. Moussa played 34 times in all competitions in his debut season at the Club, including four appearances in the Champions League.

CHRISTIAN ERIKSEN

The Danish international enjoyed his best season in a Spurs shirt. Christian was rightly awarded our Player of the Year – an even bigger honour given it was our final season at White Hart Lane. Christian started 36 of our 38 Premier League games, scoring eight goals and assisting many others, while playing 48 times in all competitions, netting 12 goals overall.

ERIK LAMELA

A serious hip problem restricted Erik to just 14 appearances last season. It was a huge blow for Erik and the Club as his early season form suggested he had fully adjusted to the demands of the Premier League. When fit, there is little doubt he's an important member of the squad.

HEUNG-MIN SON

'Sonny' enjoyed a superb second season at Spurs. The South Korean international scored 21 goals in 47 games. After Harry Kane's ankle injury in September, 'Sonny' moved further forward to great success. He was awarded the Premier League Player of the Month award for September and was recognised again in April. He also ended the season impressively, scoring two superb goals in our stunning 6-1 win over Leicester.

HARRY KANE

An incredible season from an incredible footballer. Despite two serious ankle injuries, Harry retained the Premier League's Golden Boot scoring 29 goals in just 30 appearances! That was despite having missed 11 weeks of the season through injury to make his award more remarkable. Harry's season ended in spectacular fashion, scoring eight goals in three games for Spurs. The goal scoring continued for his country, netting four in two games against Scotland and France respectively. Harry received the ultimate honour in June 2017 – the England captaincy. A perfect season for one of our own.

VINCENT JANSSEN

The Dutch international joined Spurs from AZ Alkmaar in July 2016. He endured a slow start to his Spurs career, mainly due to the form of Heung-Min Son and Harry Kane but his persistence and work rate made him a hit with the Spurs fans. Vincent scored twice in the Premier League, twice in the FA Cup and twice in the League Cup.

FERNANDO LLORENTE

Fernando joined Spurs on deadline day from Swansea City. The Spain striker signed a contract with the Club until 2019. Fernando joined Swansea from Spanish side Sevilla in August 2016, and scored 15 goals in 33 Premier League appearances last season.

THE LANE, THE FINALE

On 14th May 2017, we said a final farewell to White Hart Lane – our famous home of 118 years. The event featured former players, along with the current First Team and coaching staff and players from within the Club's Academy – marking our past, present and exciting future.

A 2-1 win over
Manchester United was a fitting
end to our wonderful stadium. It was a spine-
tingling finale as our fans sang 'Glory, Glory
Hallelujah' alongside world-renowned tenor,
Wynne Evans, accompanied by the London
Community Gospel Choir and the Tottenham
Hotspur Marching Band in what was a truly
fitting goodbye.

WATCH US RISE

SHOP SPURS

HOME OF OFFICIAL SPURS MERCHANDISE

TOTTENHAMHOTSPUR.COM/SHOP

JAN VERTONGHEN

DAVINSON SANCHEZ

It's fair to say there was a great sigh of relief and delight from Spurs supporters when it was officially announced Davinson Sanchez was a Spurs player. After a stunning season at Ajax, Davinson was linked with a number of top clubs from around Europe, but he had his heart set on a move to Spurs.

The Colombian international defender made 47 appearances for Ajax last season and won the club's 'Rinus Michels' Player of the Year Award in his only season at the club - an award previously won by Jan Vertonghen (2012) and Rafa van der Vaart (2002).

Despite being only 21 when he signed for Spurs, Sanchez was seen as the rock in an Ajax side who reached the 2017 Europa League final. Of course, Ajax were reluctant to let their star man leave, but ultimately wished him well as he departed for north London. Before joining Ajax, Davinson played for Colombian club Atletico Nacional, making 45 appearances before his move to the Netherlands. He made his professional debut for Atletico Nacional aged 17 and was part of their Copa Libertadores winning side in 2016. Having represented his country at Under-17, Under-20 and Under-23 levels, Davinson made his senior Colombia debut in November, 2016 and is now a firm fixture in the squad.

Davinson's main attributes include rapid pace and a commanding presence in defence which is an exciting prospect alongside ex-Ajax defenders Toby Alderweireld and Jan Vertonghen. Despite achieving so much in his career already, Davinson insists there's much more to come from him.

"I think everybody knows what I can become and what I can bring to the Club, such as my pace and my mental strength. I think that makes me a player that can make a big contribution for Tottenham Hotspur. This is one of the biggest clubs in the league. We can compete on any level and with any team. We're going to be aspiring to achieve big things. The project is very interesting and being able to work with players of this calibre gives you an opportunity to develop individually too. I think that when the whole group improves, so too do the individuals."

WORDSEARCH

Can you find the names of EIGHT Spurs current & former strikers from 1992 onwards in this wordsearch? Words can go horizontally, vertically and diagonally.

```
Q  H  C  U  O  R  C  L  N  N  E
S  K  H  J  L  W  H  B  E  H  N
H  T  L  Q  K  N  Q  S  N  T  A
E  K  H  I  C  K  S  X  N  V  E
R  Z  V  L  N  N  O  D  X  X  K
I  Y  R  N  A  S  Q  D  T  K  M
N  T  N  J  L  D  M  R  I  N  Y
G  L  Y  N  E  G  L  A  N  M  D
H  R  M  F  L  B  T  N  N  H  G
A  R  O  F  W  N  N  K  A  N  E
M  E  L  X  T  H  V  F  X  T  K
```

CROUCH	JANSSEN
DEFOE	KEANE
KANE	MIDO
KLINSMANN	SHERINGHAM

Answers on page 60 and 61.

KYLE WALKER-PETERS

What a summer for Kyle Walker-Peters! From Under-20 World Cup winner with England, a Man of the match Premier League debut, to a new contract.

Featuring primarily at right-back for us but also capable of playing at left-back, his moment to remember came against Newcastle on the opening day of the season. After Kieran Trippier picked up an ankle injury a week before the match, Mauricio Pochettino decided to give Kyle his league debut and he didn't disappoint, picking up the Man of the Match award!

Despite his rapid rise to the First Team, Kyle quickly pointed out his childhood as the reason for his success at Spurs.

"I'm over the moon at the moment. It was great to sign a new contract and commit my future to the Club. You don't expect to receive the man of the match on your debut, it's very different to the Under-23s but it was a great feeling."

Kyle insists whatever future success he achieves, he'll always remember where it all began.

"I used to play for Winchmore Hill as a young boy and (with mates) literally on the street in and around Tottenham. We never went to the park, we used to use people's hedges as goals. To be fair, luckily, my neighbours knew who I was and knew that I really did enjoy playing football, so a lot of the time they let me off!"

Despite the excitement and euphoria of a new signing, a supporter always takes great pride in a local academy product making it through to the First Team and Kyle echoes this view, too.

"Obviously it's good for the community, to show them that someone from that area...all it takes is hard work and dedication and you can make something of yourself," he said.

"I did that with the help of my parents, Dennis and Mary. They always tried to keep me grounded and they've always made sure that I've been smart with the decisions I make. They have kept me on a good path.

"My dad always used to say 'education before football' which I guess is a good foundation to have because things like that are important and once you've got that right, you push that to the side and then you can really focus on your football."

Kyle has simple goals for 2018 – continue to develop under Mauricio Pochettino and establish himself in the England Under-21 side. His Man of the Match award placed safely in his home, Kyle is targeting more success at the Club he loves.

"You don't want to become comfortable and think, okay, I've made one appearance, I did well...I've put that appearance to the back of my mind. It's always something I'll look back on but now it's about the next appearance and to continue learning."

OUR THREE LIONS!

Kieran Trippier became the 76th Spurs player to be capped by England when he lined-up for the Three Lions against France in June 2017. You have to go all the way back to 1903 to find our first representative. Vivian Woodward played for Spurs between 1900-1909 and was also the first Spurs player to captain England. Ahead of a World Cup qualifier, England Manager Gareth Southgate handed Harry Kane the ultimate honour – the England captain's armband. A proud day for Harry and everyone at the Club.

1 - Vivian Woodward - 14/2/1903	27 - Ron Henry - 27/2/1963	53 - Ledley King - 27/3/2002
2 - Fanny Walden - 4/4/1914	28 - Alan Mullery - 9/12/1964	54 - Jermain Defoe - 31/3/2004
3 - Tommy Clay - 15/3/1920	29 - Cyril Knowles - 6/12/1967	55 - Anthony Gardner - 31/3/2004
4 - Arthur Grimsdell - 15/3/1920	30 - Martin Peters - 18/4/1970	56 - Paul Robinson - 5/6/2004
5 - Bert Bliss - 9/4/1921	31 - Martin Chivers - 3/2/1971	57 - Michael Carrick - 28/5/2005
6 - Jimmy Dimmock - 9/4/1921	32 - Ralph Coates - 12/5/1971	58 - Jermaine Jenas - 12/10/2005
7 - Bert Smith - 9/4/1921	33 - Glenn Hoddle - 22/11/1979	59 - Aaron Lennon - 3/6/2006
8 - Jimmy Seed - 21/5/1921	34 - Ray Clemence - 9/9/1981	60 - Darren Bent - 21/11/2007
9 - Frank Osbourne - 8/12/1924	35 - Steve Perryman - 2/6/1982	61 - Jonathan Woodgate - 1/6/2008
10 - George Hunt - 13/3/1933	36 - Gary Mabbutt - 13/10/1982	62 - David Bentley - 20/8/2008
11 - Willie Hall - 6/12/1933	37 - Graham Roberts - 28/5/1983	63 - Peter Crouch - 14/10/2009
12 - Arthur Rowe - 6/12/1933	38 - Gary Stevens - 17/10/1984	64 - Tom Huddlestone - 14/11/2009
13 - Walter Alsford - 6/4/1935	39 - Chris Waddle - 11/9/1985	65 - Michael Dawson - 11/8/2010
14 - Bert Sproston - 22/10/38	40 - Steve Hodge - 18/2/1987	66 - Scott Parker - 3/9/2011
15 - Ted Ditchburn - 2/12/48	41 - Clive Allen - 29/4/1987	67 - Kyle Walker - 12/11/2011
16 - Alf Ramsey - 30/11/49	42 - Terry Fenwick - 11/2/1985	68 - Jake Livermore - 15/8/2012
17 - Eddie Baily - 2/7/1950	43 - Paul Gascoigne - 14/9/1988	69 - Steven Caulker - 14/11/2012
18 - Leslie Medley - 15/11/1950	44 - Gary Lineker - 6/9/1989	70 - Andros Townsend - 11/10/2013
19 - Bill Nicholson - 19/5/1951	45 - Paul Stewart - 11/9/1991	71 - Harry Kane - 27/3/2015
20 - Arthur Willis - 3/10/51	46 - Teddy Sheringham - 29/5/1993	72 - Ryan Mason - 31/3/2015
21 - George Robb - 25/11/53	47 - Darren Anderton - 9/3/1994	73 - Dele Alli - 9/10/2015
22 - Harry Clarke - 3/4/1954	48 - Nicky Barmby - 29/3/1995	74 - Eric Dier - 13/11/2015
23 - Johnny Brooks - 14/11/1956	49 - Sol Campbell - 18/5/1996	75 - Danny Rose - 26/3/2016
24 - Bobby Smith - 8/10/1960	50 - Ian Walker - 18/5/1996	76 - Kieran Trippier - 13/6/2017
25 - Jimmy Greaves - 14/4/1962	51 - Les Ferdinand - 10/9/1997	
26 - Maurice Norman - 20/5/1962	52 - Tim Sherwood - 27/3/1999	

INTERNATIONAL SPURS

International weekend at Hotspur Way can be a quiet time with many of the team away playing for their country. As you can see, Spurs have many international players, from all over the world.

Erik Lamela – Argentina
Davinson Sanchez – Colombia

Victor Wanyama – Kenya
Serge Aurier – Ivory Coast

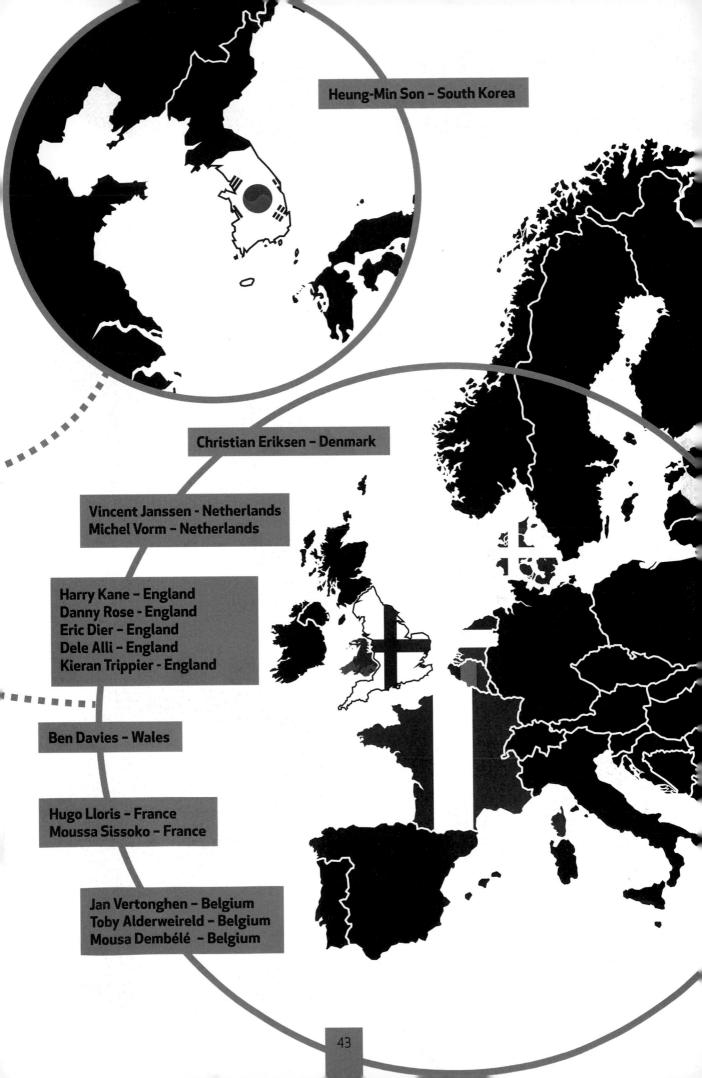

Heung-Min Son – South Korea

Christian Eriksen – Denmark

Vincent Janssen - Netherlands
Michel Vorm – Netherlands

Harry Kane – England
Danny Rose - England
Eric Dier – England
Dele Alli – England
Kieran Trippier - England

Ben Davies – Wales

Hugo Lloris – France
Moussa Sissoko – France

Jan Vertonghen – Belgium
Toby Alderweireld – Belgium
Mousa Dembélé – Belgium

MEMORY LANE

We said goodbye to our beautiful stadium as we knew it in May last year and now the excitement is building as work continues on our new 61,559 seater stadium. White Hart Lane was one of the most iconic stadiums in football and supporters have witnessed many memorable matches. Regardless of your age, you'll have a favourite moment, and we've selected four matches for every generation to enjoy!

Spurs 5-1 Arsenal – League Cup semi-final 2nd leg – 22 January 2008

It was our first win over Arsenal for nine years and to say we did it in style was an understatement. After a 1-1 draw at the Emirates, Spurs knew they had to go all out for victory and a brilliant early goal from Jermaine Jenas gave us the advantage. A Jenas free-kick came off Arsenal's Nicklas Bendtner to put us 2-0 ahead. Robbie Keane put us in control early in the second half before Aaron Lennon's clever finish put us on course for Wembley. Arsenal pulled a goal back but there was still time for Steed Malbranque to add a fifth. Spurs went on to win the League Cup, beating Chelsea 2-1 after extra-time.

Spurs 1-1 Wolves - UEFA Cup final 2nd leg - 17 May 1972

Spurs win 3-2 on aggregate

Spurs won the inaugural UEFA Cup and their second European competition, drawing 1-1 with Wolves at home after winning 2-1 at Molineux. Wearing our European all-white strip, Alan Mullery's header gave Spurs the lead. Dave Wagstaffe levelled for Wolves but Spurs held on much to the delight of the 54,000 crowd as Spurs lifted the trophy under the late, great Bill Nicholson.

Spurs 9-1 Wigan Athletic- 22 November 2009
One of those games where you can say – "I was there!"

It's remarkable to think Spurs were only leading 1-0 at half time. Nine goals were to follow, eight coming from Spurs. Jermain Defoe put Spurs 2-0 ahead after Peter Crouch's opener. Defoe was on target again on 54 minutes, before Paul Scharner pulled a goal back for Wigan. Defoe scored his hat-trick a minute later and added his fourth on 69 minutes. The crowd couldn't believe what they were watching. Defoe scored his fifth with just a few minutes remaining to put us 7-1 ahead. There was still time for two more. David Bentley's brilliant free-kick went in off Chris Kirkland and Niko Kranjcar made it Tottenham Hotspur 9 Wigan Athletic 1. We can confirm Jermain Defoe left the stadium with the match ball! It was our biggest top flight win ever and our biggest against anyone since beating Bristol Rovers 9-0 in 1977.

Spurs win UEFA Cup at the Lane…again!

Not many clubs can say they have won a major trophy in their own Stadium, but Spurs have done it twice! May 1984, Spurs fans witnessed one of the most memorable nights at White Hart Lane. Anderlecht arrived in N17 level at 1-1 after the first leg. The second leg saw a 46,000 crowd and millions watching at home on TV. It nearly ended in heartbreak as Anderlecht were ahead 2-1 on aggregate with under 10 minutes remaining, but Micky Hazard found Graham Roberts to equalise to send the game into extra time. We then won a dramatic penalty shoot-out as Tony Parks earned hero status with two penalty saves. The fans played their part in one of the Club's greatest 'Glory, Glory Nights' at The Lane.

HARRY KANE

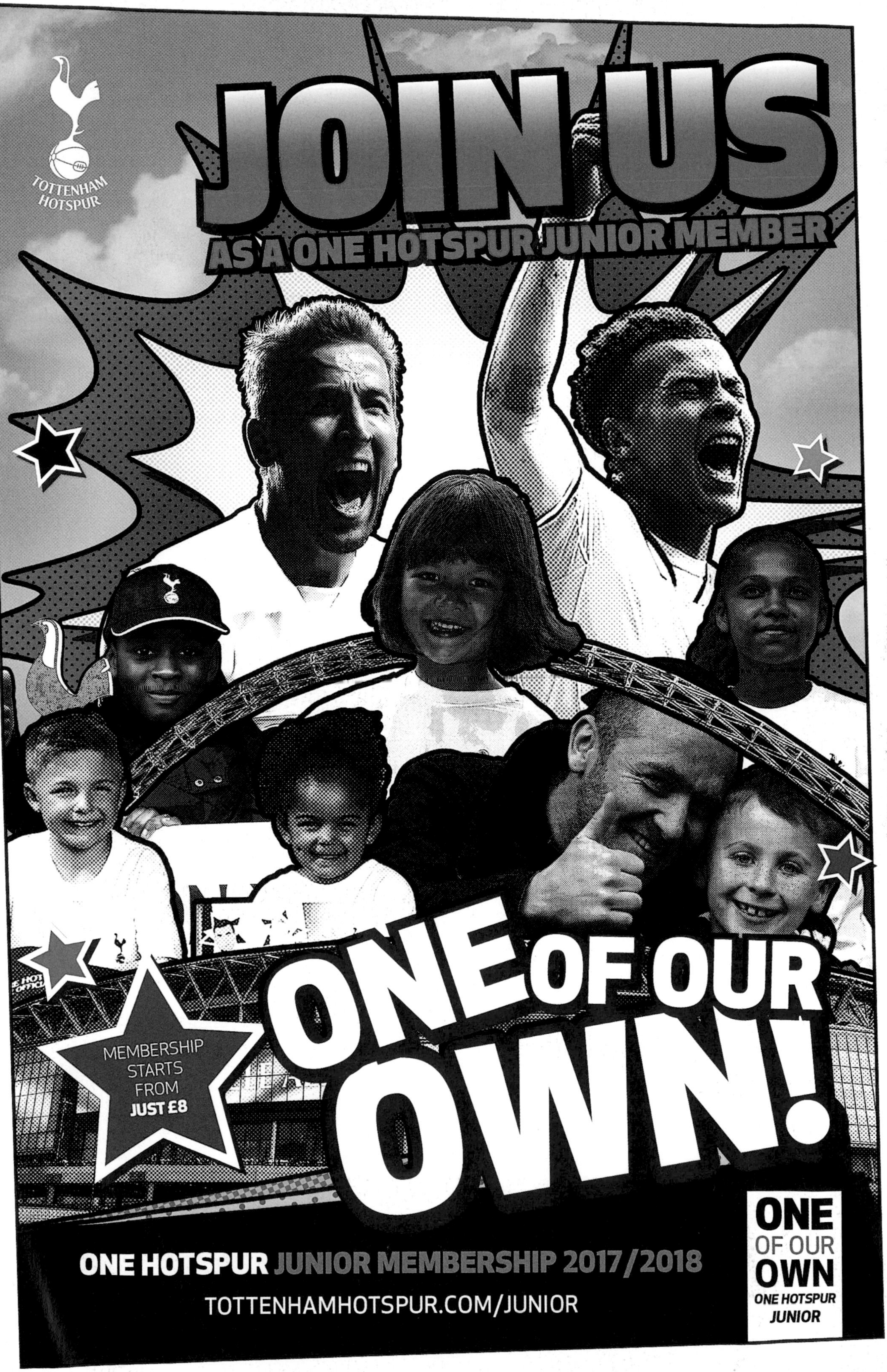
TOTTENHAM HOTSPUR
JOIN US
AS A ONE HOTSPUR JUNIOR MEMBER
MEMBERSHIP STARTS FROM JUST £8
ONE OF OUR OWN!
ONE HOTSPUR JUNIOR MEMBERSHIP 2017/2018
TOTTENHAMHOTSPUR.COM/JUNIOR
ONE OF OUR OWN
ONE HOTSPUR JUNIOR

SUPER SPURS QUIZ

It's a grand old team to play for and it's a grand old team to see, so if you know your history, try this 2018 Super Size Spurs Quiz

1 Who did we face on the opening day this season?

2 Who scored our goal of the season in 2016/2017?

3 Who did we defeat in our final match at White Hart Lane?

4 Name our Champions League group opponents.

5 Our new stadium will have a capacity of 56,000 or 61,559?

6 How many goals did Harry Kane score in the Premier League last season?

7 Name our two youngsters who won the Under-20s World Cup for England during the summer of 2017.

8 In what year did we play our first ever match at White Hart Lane?

9 Who earned his first England cap against France in June 2017?

10 On how many occasions have Spurs won the FA Cup?

11 Who did we face in our opening match at Wembley Stadium this season?

12 Name our Assistant Manager...

13 Who captained Spurs to the 1984 UEFA Cup?

14 Who scored OUR final goal at White Hart Lane?

15 How many league victories did we secure at White Hart Lane last season?

Answers on page 60

THE ULTIMATE
FOOTBALL
EXPERIENCE

TOTTENHAM
HOTSPUR
PLAYER
DEVELOPMENT

FIND OUT MORE:
tottenhamhotspur.com/soccerschools

PRE-SEASON REPORT

Spurs enjoyed another trip to the United States during pre-season including trips to Orlando, New Jersey and Nashville. Once again we were blown away by the Spurs support in the United States and look forward to returning in the near future.

Spurs 4-2 Paris St-Germain

Christian Eriksen lit up our opening International Champions Cup match with a cracker as we beat PSG 4-2 in Orlando. Christian and Eric Dier made it 2-2 at half-time, Toby Alderweireld drilled home from distance for 3-2 and Harry Kane added a late penalty in Orlando.

Spurs 2-3 Roma

Two late goals from Harry Winks and Vincent Janssen rescued us from 2-0 down against Roma, only for the Italians to find a winner in injury time in a thriller in New Jersey. Youngsters Tashan Oakley-Boothe and Anthony Georgiou also impressed off the bench.

Spurs 0-3 Manchester City

It would be hard to argue that City didn't deserve to win in front of 56,232 fans at the Nissan Stadium - a record for a soccer match in Tennessee - but it could have been different if we took our early chances, however, on this occasion, City were victorious.

Spurs 2-0 Juventus

A perfect end to pre-season as we beat the Italian double winners and Champions League finalists. Despite Juventus fielding a strong side, Spurs were comfortable throughout and were ahead after a brilliant team move ended in Kieran Trippier's perfect cross finding Harry Kane. We added a second on 52 minutes when Dele found Christian Eriksen who cooly slotted past Gianluigi Buffon.

MY CLUB - HARRY WINKS

His name is Harry and he's one of our own. We've heard that about our brilliant striker Harry Kane for a number of years now but a new local lad called Harry has emerged. Despite the euphoria of a new signing, there's nothing better than watching an Academy graduate make the grade and Harry Winks is the latest to join the First Team ranks on a regular basis. It was last season where Harry established himself in Mauricio Pochettino's squad and he hasn't looked back since. An ankle injury ended his season in early April, but after an impressive pre-season, he quickly put himself back in the forefront of the Manager's thoughts.

Born in Hemel Hempstead, Harry joined our Academy as a schoolboy aged six before signing full-time in July 2012. He signed his first professional contract two years later and his performances last season were rewarded with a new deal last February, keeping him at the Club until 2022. It was a third contract renewal inside a 12-month period, but despite the elevation, Harry has kept himself grounded and continues to learn from the likes of Mousa Dembele and Victor Wanyama. In fact, Harry found himself useful in a number of roles. Harry believes his versatility in midfield is down to his education at Academy level.

" The Academy managers throughout the years have always told me to be able to be versatile in midfield as opposed to just playing one role so, for me, if I'm on the pitch then I can adapt to what I need to do. I've had a lot of game time over the past 18 months and it's been everything I've wished for, but ultimately football can change and I need to keep that level of work rate, keep that work ethic up and keep myself going in the future. "

One of Harry's most memorable moments of his career came in November 2016, after scoring his first goal for the Club against West Ham at White Hart Lane. His first reaction was to run to Mauricio Pochettino, a Manager he describes as 'brilliant'.

" Obviously as young Academy players, all we want is opportunities and the fact that he's actually given me that and he's gradually brought me into the team, I'm very, very grateful for. He's given me my chance and put me into the First Team. The celebration was a "thank you" to him for everything he's done for me. "

From kicking a ball on a cruise ship at four years of age to starting for Spurs, there are plenty more chapters yet to be written in the exciting story of Harry Winks, one of our own…

" I've no doubt he can go right to the top. "

Scott Parker on Harry Winks

HUGO LLORIS

SPURS GROUP CHAT!

We've had a look at a Spurs group chat on a phone, but we've lost the names to the numbers! Messages were sent before we flew to the United States last summer. Can you help identify the players?

PLAYER 1:
Guys, can you recommend any good movies to watch on the plane?

PLAYER 2:
You still haven't returned my DVD from England duty!

PLAYER 1:
Sorry mate, I was a bit overwhelmed in Paris. I forgot the DVD in the hotel room. It was my first cap after all! I'll buy you another one!

PLAYER 3:
You should just try and sleep on the plane.

PLAYER 4:
Why is it so easy for you to sleep on a plane?

PLAYER 3:
I fly a lot for my international team and it's always a very long journey, unlike you European boys!

PLAYER 2:
You can watch all my goals from last season if you like: ☺ I'm Mr Goal of the Season.

PLAYER 3:
You have me to thank for a lot of your goals!

PLAYER 4:
I'm buzzing for this trip! I haven't played for ages after my injury.

PLAYER 1:
It's a big year for you, mate. You're only young, though. You might join me in the England squad one day.

PLAYER 4:
I hope so! My first priority is to be a first team regular for the team I supported as a boy!

PLAYER 2:
Right, boys, we're taking off!

Who are the players?

Player 1:

Player 2:

Player 3:

Player 4:

Answers on page 60.

PASSPORT PROBLEMS

We're just about to fly out of the country for a Champions League tie but we've left EIGHT passports at the training ground. Can you help identify the players?

<<<SPURS<<<<<<<<<<<<<<<<<<<<<<<<<
00000000000000001<<<<<<<<<<<<<

TOTTENHAM HOTSPUR F.C. - PASSPORT 1

Given Name
_____

Surname
_____

Nationality
English

Issue Date (Signed)
15/01/1994

A.

<<<SPURS<<<<<<<<<<<<<<<<<<<<<<<<<<
0000000000000000001<<<<<<<<<<<<<<

TOTTENHAM HOTSPUR F.C. - PASSPORT 2

Given Name
_____

Surname
_____

Nationality
French

Issue Date (Signed)
26/12/1986

B.

TOTTENHAM HOTSPUR F.C. - PASSPORT 3

Given Name
_____

Surname
_____

Nationality
Belgian

Issue Date (Signed)
02/03/1989

C.

TOTTENHAM HOTSPUR F.C. - PASSPORT 4

Given Name
_____

Surname
_____

Nationality
South Korean

Issue Date (Signed)
28/08/2015

D.

<<<SPURS<<<<<<<<<<<<<<<<<<
00000000000000001<<<<<<<<

TOTTENHAM HOTSPUR F.C. - PASSPORT 5

Given Name
_____

Surname
_____

Nationality
Kenyan

Issue Date (Signed)
28/08/2015

E.

<<<SPURS<<<<<<<<<<<<<<<<<<
00000000000000001<<<<<<<<

TOTTENHAM HOTSPUR F.C. - PASSPORT 6

Given Name
_____

Surname
_____

Nationality
Welsh

Issue Date (Signed)
23/07/2014

F.

<<<SPURS<<<<<<<<<<<<<<<<<<
00000000000000001<<<<<<<<

TOTTENHAM HOTSPUR F.C. - PASSPORT 7

Given Name
_____

Surname
_____

Nationality
Dutch

Issue Date (Signed)
12/07/2016

G.

<<<SPURS<<<<<<<<<<<<<<<<<<
00000000000000001<<<<<<<<

TOTTENHAM HOTSPUR F.C. - PASSPORT 8

Given Name
_____

Surname
_____

Nationality
English

Issue Date (Signed)
01/07/2009

H.

Answers on page 60 & 61.

WHITE HART LANE RECORDS

Our 118-year stay at the White Hart Lane as we knew it is over, so let's look back on the stats, facts and figures you might have missed.

	P	W	D	L	F	A	GD	PTS
Southern League (1899-1908)	147	104	25	18	334	107	227	233
FL/PL (1908-2017)	1993	1102	462	429	3983	2326	1657	3036
FA Cup (1900-2017)	193	124	46	23	472	189	283	N/A
League Cup (1968-2017)	105	71	15	19	234	100	134	N/A
Europe (1961-2016)	95	70	18	7	246	71	175	N/A
TOTALS	2533	1471	566	496	5269	2793	2476	3269

First Football League game
01.09.1908 v Wolves, Division Two (W3-0)

Last Football League game
25.04.1992 v Everton, Division One (D3-3)

First Premier League game
19.08.1992 v Coventry City (L0-2)

Last Premier League game
14.05.2017 v Manchester United (W2-1)

First FA Cup game
08.02.1901 v Preston North End, first round (D1-1)

Last FA Cup game
12.03.2017 v Millwall, quarter-final (W6-0)

First League Cup game
25.09.1968 v Exeter City, third round (W6-3)

Last League Cup game
21.09.2016 v Gillingham, third round (W5-0)

First European game
20.09.1961 v Gornik Zabrze, European Cup, preliminary round, second leg (W8-1

Last European game
17.03.2016 v Borussia Dortmund, Europa League, Round of 16, second leg (L1-2)

Most goals scored at White Hart Lane

176 – Jimmy Greaves (1961-1970)
130 – Bobby Smith (1955-1963)
111 – Martin Chivers (1967-1980)
106 – Cliff Jones (1957-1968)
102 – Len Duquemin (1946-1957)
91 – George Hunt (1930-1937)
90 – Jermain Defoe (2004-2014)
86 – Alan Gilzean (1964-1975)
79 – Bert Bliss (1911-1923)
76 – Les Bennett (1939-1955)

QUIZ AND PUZZLE ANSWERS

P37 WORD SEARCH

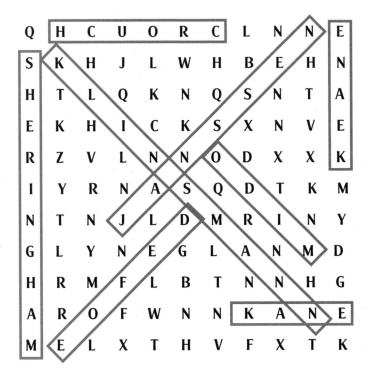

P48 SUPER SPURS QUIZ

1 Newcastle
2 Dele Alli
3 Manchester United
4 Scott Parker
5 61,559
6 29
7 Kyle Walker-Peters
8 1899
9 Kieran Trippier
10 8
11 Chelsea
12 Jesus Perez
13 Graham Roberts
14 Harry Kane
15 17 out of 19

P54 SPURS GROUP CHAT!

PLAYER 1 – TRIPPIER
PLAYER 2 – DELE ALLI
PLAYER 3 – HEUNG-MIN SON
PLAYER 4 – HARRY WINKS

P56 PASSPORT PROBLEMS

A. ERIC DIER
B. HUGO LLORIS
C. TOBY ALDERWEIRELD
D. HEUNG-MIN SON
E. VICTOR WANYAMA
F. BEN DAVIES
G. VINCENT JANSSEN
H. HARRY KANE

MOUSA DEMBELE

WHERE'S CHIRPY?